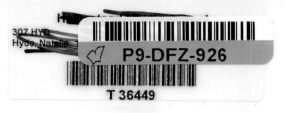

POPULATION PATTERNS

What factors determine the location and growth of human settlements?

By Natalie Hyde

Crabtree Publishing Company

www.crabtreebooks.com

Author: Natalie Hyde
Project director: Ruth Owen
Designer: Elaine Wilkinson
Editors: Mark Sachner, Lynn Peppas
Editorial director: Kathy Middleton
Prepress technician: Katherine Berti
Production coordinator: Margaret Amy Salter
Consultant: Ceri Oeppen BSc, MSc, of the Sussex Centre for Migration Research

Developed & Created for Crabtree Publishing Company by Ruby Tuesday Books Ltd

Front cover (top): The city of Cairo, in Egypt, has been the site of major settlements for thousands of years due to its proximity to the Nile River.
Front cover (bottom left): An aerial view of suburban streets.
Front cover (bottom center): The Cliff Palace of the Anasazi people in Colorado.
Front cover (bottom right): The fishing village of Mevagissey in Cornwall, United Kingdom.
Back cover: A huge suburban housing development in Calgary, Alberta, Canada.
Title page: Kuala Lumpur, the capital of Malaysia, may be seen looming over the urban sprawl that has developed as suburbs and commuter towns beyond the city's original boundaries.

Photo credits:
Alamy: Walter Bibikow: pages 5 (top), 6–7 (top), 6 (bottom); Victor Paul Borg: pages 9 (bottom), 14–15 (center); Gary Cook: pages 17 (top), 22–23 (center), 22 (top); Stefan Auth: page 25 (top); Ludwig M Brinckmann: pages 28 (center), 30–31 (center), 32–33 (center); Rolf Hicker: pages 35, 36–37 (center); Lee Thomas: page 39 (bottom)
Corbis: Lewis Wickes Hine: page 31 (top); Nik Wheeler: pages 32 (bottom), 34 (bottom)
Cosmographics: page 10 (bottom)
Getty Images: Victor Englebert: page 7 (bottom); Billy Stickland: pages 11 (bottom), 18 (top)
Ruby Tuesday Books Ltd: front cover (bottom right), pages 4 (bottom), 8 (bottom), 9 (top), 12 (bottom)
Science Photo Library: page 13
Shutterstock: front cover (top, bottom left, bottom center), pages 3 (right center), 3 (right), 4 (left), 5 (bottom), 8 (left), 10 (top), 11 (center), 13 (bottom all), 14 (left), 15 (top left), 15 (top right), 16 (top), 16 (bottom), 17 (bottom), 18–19 (center), 19 (top), 19 (center), 20 (left top), 20 (bottom), 21 (bottom), 22 (top), 26 (left), 27, 28–29 (center), 29 (bottom), 33 (bottom), 32 (left), 37 (top), 39 (top), 40–41 (center)
Wikipedia (public domain): back cover, pages 1, 3 (left), 3 (left center), 12 (top), 20 (left bottom), 21 (top), 24 (top), 24–25 (center), 26 (bottom), 33 (top), 37 (bottom), 38, 40 (left), 41 (top), 42–43

Library and Archives Canada Cataloguing in Publication

Hyde, Natalie, 1963-
   Population patterns : what factors determine the location and growth of human settlements? / Natalie Hyde.

(Investigating human migration & settlement)
Includes index.
ISBN 978-0-7787-5182-3 (bound).--ISBN 978-0-7787-5197-7 (pbk.)

   1. Population geography--History--Juvenile literature. 2. Human settlements--Juvenile literature. 3. Land use--Economic aspects--Juvenile literature. 4. Cities and towns--Growth--Juvenile literature.
I. Title. II. Series: Investigating human migration & settlement

HB1951.H93 2010   j304.6   C2009-905269-5

Library of Congress Cataloging-in-Publication Data

Hyde, Natalie, 1963-
 Population patterns : what factors determine the location and growth of human settlements? / by Natalie Hyde.
    p. cm. -- (Investigating human migration & settlement)
 Includes index.
 ISBN 978-0-7787-5197-7 (pbk. : alk. paper) -- ISBN 978-0-7787-5182-3 (reinforced library binding : alk. paper)
 1. Population geography--History--Juvenile literature. 2. Land use--Economic aspects--Juvenile literature. 3. Cities and towns--Growth--Juvenile literature. I. Title.
 HB1951.H923 2010
 307--dc22

                                                2009034887

Crabtree Publishing Company

www.crabtreebooks.com   1-800-387-7650

Printed in China/122009/CT20090915

Published in Canada
Crabtree Publishing
616 Welland Ave.
St. Catharines, ON
L2M 5V6

Published in the United States
Crabtree Publishing
PMB 59051
350 Fifth Avenue, 59th Floor
New York, New York 10118

Published in the United Kingdom
Crabtree Publishing
Maritime House
Basin Road North, Hove
BN41 1WR

Published in Australia
Crabtree Publishing
386 Mt. Alexander Rd.
Ascot Vale (Melbourne)
VIC 3032

CONTENTS

▼ Tourists and photographers come to Yuanyang in China to see the beautiful landscapes created by the terraced rice fields, which date back 2,500 years and are still in use today.

PATTERNS OF MIGRATION & SETTLEMENT

Humans have been on the move for thousands and thousands of years. Scientists believe that 170,000 years ago, early modern humans—our ancestors *Homo sapiens sapiens*—developed in Africa. About 150,000 years ago, they began to migrate around that continent. In time, their migrations took them around the world.

The Needs of Early Settlements

No matter where humans settled, they had the same basic needs—water, a constant source of food, and shelter. As humans became more advanced, they developed new needs. They settled in places where there was a

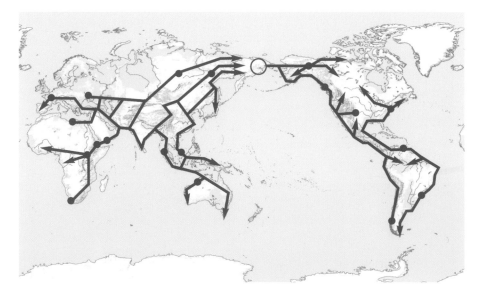

▲ This map shows the routes that historians believe early modern humans took throughout the period from 150,000 years ago to 10,000 years ago to settle Europe, Asia, North America, South America, and Australia.

◄ In developing nations such as India and the Philippines, many large cities have become home to call centers. These operations offer customer support to banking, credit card, and electronics corporations based in Europe and North America. Employment opportunities in call centers have attracted many young, educated people, and their numbers have added significant growth to the population of many cities in India. Here, workers are on their way to call center jobs in HITEC City in Andhra Pradesh, India.

NOMADS: PEOPLE ON THE MOVE

Some groups do not settle in one place at all. They roam over vast areas, carrying their belongings with them as they move. Many of these nomads live in areas with a harsh climate or difficult growing conditions, such as deserts, high mountains, or dense rain forests. These people move often, following the seasons and sources of food and water.

The Bedouin are nomads who have traditionally lived in deserts in North Africa and the Middle East, including the Sahara, Sinai, Arabian, and Negev deserts, herding goats and sheep.

In the last half of the 1900s, many Bedouin groups started taking jobs—and settling—in cities throughout the Middle East, particularly when the onset of droughts reduced the availability of land they had used to graze their livestock.

source of wood for fuel and for building shelters, or rock for construction. They settled where the land was fertile and the climate was suitable for growing crops. In ancient China, for example, farmers in Yuanyang built terraced rice fields into the sides of mountains to take advantage of the climate at certain heights.

Settlements Today

Historically, most population patterns could be determined by such factors as the availability of water and other natural resources, or by the proximity to sources of income from the natural world, such as coal, gold, or animal products. Those factors are still important today, but the availability of human resources for jobs in computer, communications, and customer-care sectors are equally as important, too.

Throughout history and even today, settlements that have developed as places where businesses can grow—and where jobs may be found— have also grown into cities and towns. This is true of most North American cities, particularly those that grew up into centers of commerce along the sea coasts, the Great Lakes, and major rivers, where water served as both a source of power and a means of transportation.

Today, in most parts of the world, a similar phenomenon is occurring. In India, for example, the growth of industry in cities such as Thane has

▲ Bedouin groups have traditionally traveled from one oasis to another, living in tents that can be dismantled and carried on the backs of camels.

created districts that have brought people to work in factories and created the need for building, transportation, and other services, which lead to more jobs. In larger cities, such as Mumbai and Kolkata, the rising and falling fortunes of industry have affected population growth. In more recent years, population growth has also been affected by the rapid rise of computer and information technology industries.

Settlement and Adaptation to Environments

Today humans have settled in many different environments in nearly every part of the world. People who have settled in extreme environments xhave adapted to live in these places.

▼ *Trees do not grow in the high Arctic, so Inuit people found other ways to build shelters. In the summer many lived in tents made of caribou skins. In the winter they built igloos. The thick snow walls protected them from the biting winds and freezing temperatures. Today, most Inuit live in modern housing. They still use traditional shelters such as tipis and igloos while traveling and hunting.*

◄ *Coober Pedy, Australia, is known as the "Opal Capital of the World." Its name is an English version of the Aboriginal words "kupa piti" which mean "white man in a hole." Aborigines are the indigenous people of Australia.*

Inuit and the High Arctic

Many Inuit people of northern Canada, along with other Native people in Alaska, Greenland, and Siberia in the far northeast of Russia, live along the coast of the Arctic Sea. Their ancestors settled here to be near the whales, seals, and caribou that were their main diet. The earlier people who settled here became experts at hunting larger sea mammals, and many people still hunt these and other Arctic animals today. One good hunt would mean the entire community would have plenty of food for a long time. The animals also provided oil for lamps and skins for clothing and shelter.

In the 1300s, during a period when temperatures were slightly lower than usual in the Arctic, many Native people in this region migrated to the southern subarctic regions. Inuit and other Native people still inhabit milder subarctic regions today, but many have returned to the high Arctic where they had originally made their homes.

Adapting to the Heat of the Australian Outback

Coober Pedy is a small town in the outback of southern Australia. In 1915, prospectors looking for gold found the gemstone opal in the area. A mining settlement soon sprang up that, over the following decades, would attract migrants of many nationalities eager to make their fortune.

The Australian outback is a desert environment, and the area around Coober Pedy receives just five inches (12.7 centimeters) of rain each year. Summer temperatures can reach 113 degrees F (45 degrees C) in the shade. The settlers of Coober Pedy have adapted to living in this extreme climate by living underground, where the temperature stays cool and comfortable. The town has homes, or "dugouts" as they are called by locals, stores, a church, and even swimming pools built underground! Today, Coober Pedy has 3,500 residents from 45 different nationalities and attracts thousands of tourists who come to see this unique settlement.

▶ *Most of the Yanomamo people's family and village life takes place in the communal shabono, shown here.*

LIFE IN THE RAIN FOREST

The Yanomamo people live in a large area of the rain forest of Brazil and Venezuela, in South America.

The Yanomamo live in small communities similar to what other cultures would call villages. Each community lives in one large communal home called a *shabono*. Only the edges of the oval structure have a roof, and the center of the shabono is where people can meet for group activities. The shabono makes use of the abundance of materials available in the rain forest, including tree trunks, vines, and leaves. The shabono is not very sturdy and is often damaged by storms and insects, and it needs to be rebuilt every one or two years.

The Yanomamo hunt animals and fish, gather fruit, and grow bananas.

CHAPTER TWO

EARLY HUMAN MIGRATIONS

The first people to migrate faced many challenges. They did not have roads, bridges, or tunnels to get around natural obstacles such as mountains, rivers, or seas. The landscape influenced where they settled.

Out of Africa—Migrating Across the Sahara

Deserts also formed a natural barrier to travel. Our earliest ancestors—those from whom we are believed to have directly descended as modern humans—are thought to have first appeared in Africa about 170,000 years ago. These early modern humans moved around the sub-Saharan regions of Africa for tens of thousands of years before actually leaving Africa. They did not have any way to cross the large, dry Sahara Desert. Many scientists believe that about 125,000 years ago a shift occurred in Africa's climate. A milder and wetter climate allowed rivers to form in the north, and the desert sands turned into a vast grassland. With plenty of wild animals to hunt, people could make the journey north and east.

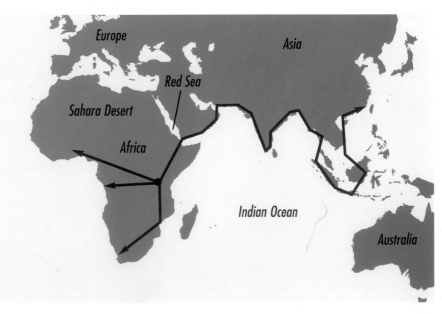

▲ The route taken by early migrants out of Africa around 85,000 years ago.

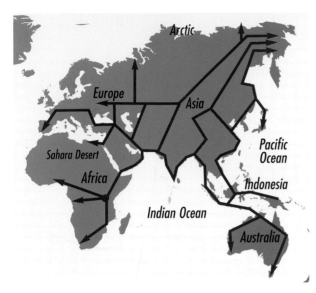

◄ Scientific evidence indicates that about 25,000 years ago, humans had migrated into Europe as far west as present-day Spain and France, as far north as the Arctic regions of Eurasia, the Indonesian archipelago of islands, and into Australia and other island areas of the South Pacific.

Archaeologists have found evidence that they crossed the Sinai Peninsula out of Africa and into the Middle East.

Around 115,000 years ago, the climate had become colder and drier, and the Sahara began to reassert itself again as desert. The rivers dried up, and the herds moved south. Scientific research suggests that 90,000 years ago those people who had migrated to the Middle East had died out and the route out of Africa had closed up again.

Out of Africa—Across the Red Sea

Scientists believe that about 85,000 years ago, another group of humans migrated out of Africa and into the Middle East—this time along a more southern route across the mouth of the Red Sea and along the southern shore of the Arabian Peninsula. It is believed that all non-African people are descended from this group. From the Middle East, their migrations took them across the southern coast of the Asian continent, including the vast mass of the Indian subcontinent, and across the coastal regions surrounding the Indian Ocean.

Over tens of thousands of years of periodic warming, cooling, and freezing in various parts of the planet, humans made their way across southern and southeastern Asia, up along the eastern Asian coast, back toward India and the Middle East, and up into central Asia and southern and eastern Europe. With the approach of a period of extreme cold, the face of the planet and of human settlement would also enter a new phase.

ANCIENT GRAFFITI

Early humans left behind a history in pictures. Pictographs are paintings made with early types of "paint," for example, crushed rock called red ochre. Petroglyphs are pictures carved into rock using stone tools. Ancient rock art in the Sahara Desert has shown scientists a very different environment than the desert we know today. Images of giraffes, buffalos, elephants, ostriches, and large antelope decorate rocks and cliffs. Humans are often shown much smaller than the animals and carry boomerangs, clubs, axes, or bows. There are also petroglyphs of fish, crocodiles, and hippos, showing that there were once ancient rivers and lakes in the area.

▼ These petroglyphs found in the Sahara show wildlife living in the desert during an age when the region could sustain large numbers of animals.

9

▼ *Using the scientific description of an ice age, it can be said that Earth is still in an ice age now. Large areas around the polar regions are covered with ice and snow, much of it in the form of huge ice sheets called glaciers. In this photo, a glacier is retreating, and it is possible to see how glaciers form landscape features such as valleys.*

Ice Ages

Even as "recently" as tens of thousands of years ago, our planet did not look as it does today. Throughout its existence, Earth has gone through periods of warmer and colder weather. Periods known as ice ages have occurred for millions of years, starting back when many of the planet's physical features were still forming. During an ice age, significant parts of Earth's surface are covered by ice.

Glacial Periods

Within the ice ages were periods of more extreme cold, called glacial periods. These periods usually lasted for thousands of years. The latest such glacial period is thought to have begun at least 26,000 years ago and ended 13,000 years ago. During that time glaciers moved over vast stretches of North America and northern Eurasia. Since then, the glaciers have retreated, leaving behind their impact on the soil,

▲ *The 45th parallel north is a point halfway between the equator and the North Pole. It is considered to be the southernmost extent of glaciation in the most recent glacial period. Geological features such as the Great Lakes and Niagara Falls were carved out during this time.*

water reserves, and landscape of vast regions of the Northern Hemisphere. These glacial regions extended as far south as the circle of latitude known as the 45th parallel north.

The glaciers and their aftermath also had an effect on patterns of human migration.

"Land Bridges" and Other Migratory Routes

During these glacial periods, so much of the planet's water was locked in glacial ice that the sea levels dropped. This meant that continents became larger as the continental shelf, which would normally be undersea, became exposed as dry land.

Land that had been underwater was uncovered and created formations that are commonly referred to as "land bridges." These formations, some of which may have been hundreds of miles wide, allowed people and animals to cross into new continents. Plants also slowly spread from one continent to another.

Once Earth's climate began warming and the glaciers began melting —a gradual process that is believed to have begun about 13,000 years ago—sea levels rose again. Slowly this caused these "land bridges" to once more be underwater. People and animals that had migrated were now cut off from returning.

Papua New Guinea

Land bridge

Australia

◀ Some scientists believe that between 60,000 and 30,000 years ago a land bridge — in the area indicated on the map — allowed humans to cross from southeast Asia into Australia.

A "LAND BRIDGE" TO AUSTRALIA?

Scientists believe that a "land bridge" may have connected New Guinea to Australia, and Borneo to Sumatra. This left a gap of open sea about 62 miles (100 km) wide. At some point, humans are believed to have made the crossing from southeast Asia into Australia. The exact years of the earliest migrations into Australia are not certain. Most estimates range from 60,000 to 30,000 years ago, and it is thought that some migrants may have "island hopped" in small boats as well as on foot. Once Earth warmed again, the sea levels rose with maximum levels most likely reached about 6,000 years ago. Australia went back to being what it had been about 50 million years ago when it broke off from Antarctica — a geographically isolated continent with many unique species of animals and plants.

◀ The indigenous Aborigine people are officially recognized by the government of Australia as descended from the first human inhabitants of Australia. Here, Cathy Freeman of Australia wins the gold medal in the 400 meters at the 2000 Olympic Games in Sydney. Freeman was only the second Aboriginal athlete in history to win an Olympic gold medal.

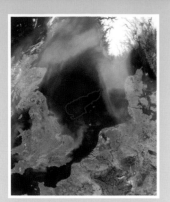

A "LAND BRIDGE" TO GREAT BRITAIN?

Archaeologists have found traces of early humans in England, suggesting that it was once linked to the rest of Europe. Trawlers working off the coast of the Netherlands have dragged up lion and mammoth bones as well as ancient tools and weapons. These items all support the existence of a stretch of land between Great Britain and the European continent. This area is thought to have existed as recently as 10,000–4,000 years ago. It existed long enough, and covered enough area, to have been a place of human settlement and not just a migratory path between Europe and Great Britain. Today it is now underwater beneath the North Sea. Geologists have named it Doggerland, after *dogge*, an old Dutch word for a fishing boat. The satellite image above shows Dogger Bank, a large sand bank that is the remains of Doggerland.

A "Land Bridge" to the Americas?

Most scientists agree that a large land formation once connected Siberia to Alaska starting around 25,000 years ago. Today we call that formation Beringia. Most people think of Beringia as a "land bridge" across which people migrated from Siberia to Alaska. It was actually more like a landmass—some scientists have called it a subcontinent—about 1,000 miles (1,600 km) across at its widest extent.

Between 25,000 and 13,000 years ago, the Arctic regions went through periods of warming and freezing. During warm periods, Beringia would have been covered with grasslands and provided a place for people to settle.

The First Americans

Most scientists believe that the first "true" Americans—and the ancestors of Native people in the Americas today—migrated across Beringia from Siberia. For a period of several thousand years the Arctic went through a "deep freeze" and the migrants were blocked from their progress by glaciers in North America. Once the Arctic warmed up enough for the glaciers to retreat, people continued their migration and eventually populated all of North, Central, and South America.

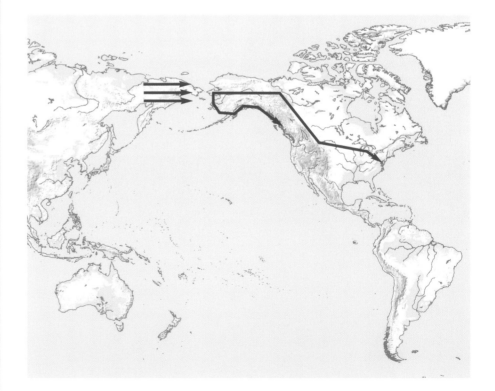

▲ *This map shows the route that many scientists believe was taken by early humans in order to settle the Americas around 25,000 to 20,000 years ago.*

▲ It is believed that the people who migrated and settled on Beringia or crossed over into Alaska were hunter-gatherers. Siberian hunters would have followed herds of reindeer, musk ox, and wooly mammoths across this land formation.

There have been several theories about other possible origins and migrations of early Americans. The idea that people may have lived in parts of South America 30,000 years ago or more, is based on artifacts and archaeological evidence. These theories, based on the characteristics of human remains found in these regions, suggest that there is a stronger resemblance to aboriginal people who inhabited Australia, rather than to those who migrated across Beringia.

Theories based on this evidence suggest that early Americans may have migrated by sea or over other prehistoric land connections in the southern hemisphere. These theories are hotly debated, especially when held up against the widely held view that all Native Americans are descended from those who came across Beringia.

◄ All of the people shown here belong to Native tribes and nations of the Americas. Are they all descended from a common group that migrated from Siberia to Alaska? Or is the ethnic makeup of Native people more varied than previously thought with roots in the Americas that go back farther than has commonly been believed?

FOCUS ON:

MOUNTAIN MIGRATORY ROADBLOCKS— THE PAMIR KNOT

Along with hot, dry deserts and large bodies of water, huge mountain ranges formed roadblocks for early migrants. The Pamir Mountains, also known as the Pamir Knot and the "Roof of the World," are in the present-day central Asian nation of Tajikistan where four different mountain ranges meet. When humans first came into this area— probably about 40,000 years ago— this junction forced land travelers to go either north into central Asia or south into what are now Pakistan and India. The Pamirs have long been one of the most forbidding and difficult regions to navigate as both a trade route and a place of human settlement. Nevertheless, several roads wind their way through the mountains, and various Central Asian groups have lived throughout the region, most of them in farming settlements.

▼ The city of Cairo, which sits on the Nile River, is the capital of Egypt and the largest city in the Arab world. The city of Cairo was founded in the 900s, but this location has been the site of major settlements for thousands of years due to its proximity to the river and the fertile Nile delta.

CHAPTER THREE

LANDSCAPE & CLIMATE

Our earliest ancestors were influenced in their migrations by conditions affecting the land and climate on a grand scale. Just as landscape and climate were major factors in the prehistoric migrations of modern humans, so have they also played an important part in more recent migration and settlement patterns.

For the Love of Water

Historic and scientific evidence, ancient writings—even the very existence of some of the world's largest and most important cities today—have all shown that in both ancient and modern times, people have sought out and settled alongside bodies of water. Rivers in particular have historically been

▲ *Four hundred million people live along the banks of the Ganges River, making it one of the busiest, most densely populated, and most polluted rivers in the world. Here, people gather to bathe in the river at the holy city of Varanasi.*

▼ *Apart from Jericho's religious significance as a place along the Jordan River, the sources of food and water in Jericho have made it a very attractive place to settle. Here, archaeologists uncover the layers of Jericho's past.*

a draw to migrants in search of fresh water for drinking, cooking, and food. In addition to providing an abundant source of fish, lakes and streams have long been desirable places to hunt animals coming to drink. For many cultures of the world, rivers have also had a spiritual significance, drawing people to visit, pray, celebrate, and settle along their banks.

Jericho—An Ancient Biblical Site

Jericho is located along the Jordan River in the West Bank. With evidence of settlement dating back 11,000 years, Jericho is one of the oldest continuously inhabited cities in the world. Archaeologists have found the ruins of 20 different settlements on the same site in Jericho. Described throughout ancient religious texts as being surrounded by palm trees and having many springs, today the city has at least one spring that produces almost 1,000 gallons (4,000 liters) of water per minute. This water is used to help irrigate land used to grow crops.

India's Holy River

The Ganges River in India has long been important for reasons other than simply as a source of food and transportation. Believing that bathing in the river can wash away a person's sins, about two million Hindus bathe in the Ganges each day. There are also hundreds of temples along its banks, especially in the holy city of Varanasi. The many religious festivals celebrated along the river bring even more people to the area.

The Ganges starts in the western Himalaya Mountains and, at the end of its 1,560-mile (2,510-km) journey, it empties into the Indian Ocean. Besides being important for religious reasons, the Ganges is also an important source of water for washing clothes and cooking.

Depending on the Nile

Ancient Egypt would not have grown into such a large and powerful nation without the Nile River. Around the Nile is dry and empty desert, but the land on either side of the river is lush and green. Egyptians depended on the yearly flooding of the Nile to improve the land. Yearly flooding would spread rich silt on flat flood plains, making the soil more fertile.

The ancient Egyptians were excellent farmers. They knew the best crops to grow and when and where to plant them. They dug irrigation channels to help bring water to even more land for growing crops. The population was able to grow quickly because they were able to grow and store so much food. With plenty of well-fed workers, the pharaohs could build incredible structures such as tombs, temples, and pyramids.

The Egyptians also built the first known ships. They had flat-bottomed boats they used for sailing up and down the Nile and ships for sailing on the Red Sea. The abundant crops made Egypt a wealthy civilization by providing flax and wheat to trade with

▲ This satellite image of the Nile River shows its banks as a strip of lush green in stark contrast to the dry desert in this part of North Africa.

▼ This rural mosque on the banks of the Nile River is surrounded by productive gardens filled with strong, healthy crops that are irrigated with water from the river.

FOCUS ON:

AQUEDUCTS THEN AND NOW

Cities need a steady supply of water to grow. If the city is in an area that is not near a spring or river, a new source of water must be found. The Romans found a way to bring water to large cities across their empire. They built aqueducts out of stone. Aqueducts are water bridges that transport water from rivers or mountains into settlements. The Pont du Gard in France (seen below) is a Roman aqueduct built over 2,000 years ago to bring water to the town of Nimes. Aqueducts are still in use today. The Hayden-Rhodes Aqueduct in Arizona brings water from the Colorado River to many towns and cities such as Phoenix and Tucson.

▲ *This is the "solar boat" of Pharaoh Khufu that was found close to the pharaoh's tomb, the Great Pyramid at Giza. Scientists believe that the ancient Egyptians carried ship pieces all the way to the coast and then assembled the ship in the place where they would set sail from.*

other nations that faced starvation due to droughts.

Archaeologists have also found two boats in pieces near the Great Pyramid. These boats were made and buried for the entombed pharaoh so he could travel across the sky with the sun god, Ra. Scientists have carefully put one of the boats back together. It fit together like a jigsaw puzzle. The planks were made of cedar and were not held together with nails or screws. The pieces of wood were joined with twisted plant fibers that fit inside U-shaped holes.

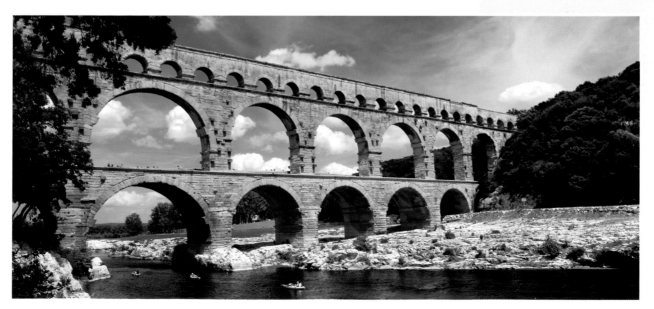

Directed by Climate

Climate also plays an important role in where people settle. Crops can only grow where there is a reasonable growing season. If the temperatures are cold many months of the year, then the plants do not have enough time to mature. If it is too hot and dry, crops will not have the water they need to flourish.

While some people have adapted well to living in very cold or very dry areas, most settlements are found in areas with warm temperatures at least half of the year and enough rain to supply them and their crops with water.

A Subtropical Climate: Tokyo

The city with the largest population in the world is Tokyo, Japan. Tokyo has a subtropical climate. This means it has hot, humid summers and mild winters. This climate is good for growing crops. Japan is a series of islands, and there is not a lot of land for farming. The warm temperatures and ample rainfall means that even small garden plots can be turned into rice paddies.

Cold, Dry, Thinly Settled

The countries with the lowest populations for their size tend to lie in colder or drier parts of the world. Mongolia has the lowest number of residents for its size. The northern part of the country is cold and mountainous. The southern part is taken up by the Gobi Desert. Mongolia has long, cold winters and short summers.

Food in Mongolia consists mostly of dairy products, meats, and fats. Mongolians do not use a lot of vegetables or spices in their cooking, as the climate does not make them easy to grow.

Mild and Densely Settled

One of the smallest countries in the world also has the highest density, or most people for its size. Monaco is

▲ *Residents and workers at the Roppongi Hills business, shopping, and residential complex in Tokyo, Japan, take part in an annual rice-planting event in a paddy field that forms part of the complex's roof garden.*

▶ *The population of Monaco, numbering just under 33,000, shares an area less than one square mile (2.6 sq km) with thousands of tourists. Originally a fortress, the tiny settlement's scenery, climate, and casino industry have turned the country into a wealthy tourist destination.*

▲ ▶ *Many Mongolian people live a nomadic life herding goats, sheep, horses, cattle, and camels. They breed Bactrian camels (above) that are able to endure the extremes, both hot and cold, of the Mongolian climate. The camels are used as beasts of burden to carry around the portable "yurt" homes used by the Mongolians. The yurt can be put up or dismantled in under an hour!*

sandwiched between France and the Mediterranean Sea. It is mild all year long with only about 60 days of rain each year. Tourism is one of Monaco's main sources of income.

Monaco is best known for its casinos and the Monaco Grand Prix. The Formula One cars snake their way through the narrow, twisting roads on one of the most difficult race courses in the world. This yearly race and the pleasant climate bring thousands of visitors to Monaco each year.

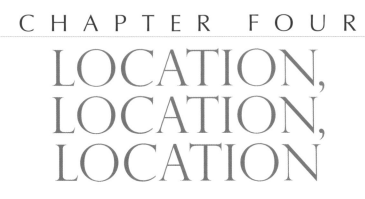

CHAPTER FOUR

LOCATION, LOCATION, LOCATION

Throughout the history of human migration and settlement, any city, town, or settlement that wasn't built to be safely distanced, protected, or defended from its enemies could be raided and destroyed. Many historical towns and cities—some ancient, others more recent—were built in places that made it difficult for them to be attacked. A hill or mountain was a wise place to locate a settlement. Being on high ground meant that residents could see a long distance. An army or attackers could not sneak up and surprise them. In addition, the difficulty of getting up a steep hill or mountain would slow invaders down.

▲ The clifftop fortress of Masada in the Judean Desert was built by King Herod between 37 and 31 BC. Some sections are over 1,400 feet (425 m) above the surrounding land.

◄ Top: Chateau Frontenac in Quebec City looks out over the St. Lawrence River in Canada. Bottom: Castle Katz overlooking the Rhine River in St. Goarshausen, Germany.

▲ The main Dogon settlement is seen here on the Bandiagara Escarpment, a vast sandstone cliff that is over 1,600 feet (480 m) high. Around one thousand years ago, the Dogon people were under threat from Muslims in their country because the Dogon would not convert to Islam. They settled on the walls of this cliff as a means of defending themselves against raids.

The View from Above—Fortresses, Castles, and Hills

Quebec City, in Canada, sits on the top of a cliff overlooking the St. Lawrence River. In the 1700s, its location helped protect citizens and troops from British soldiers who sailed up the river to attack. While the British struggled up the cliffs, the residents rained bullets down on them.

More than 25 castles tower over the Rhine River in Germany. Dating back over 1,000 years to the Middle Ages, they were built on top of the mountains that line the river valley. Shield walls, towers, and turrets helped protect the people living in and near the castles.

Rome is the city built on seven hills. It is said that seven different groups of people had settlements on each of the hills. The settlements began to hold games and other events, and over time they decided to drain the marshes in the valleys and join together to make one community. They built walls around the seven hills to protect them from enemies.

Living on the Edge

Some people built—and continue to build—settlements not just on the tops of mountains or hills but on the steep sides of them as well. Often, a river running down the side of a mountain would cut into its sides. This meant that not only were residents protected from attack, but they also had a source of water nearby.

▲ A small Dogon market in a Bandiagara village. The Dogon construct their buildings from sandstone mud.

Dogon Architecture

The Dogon are a tribe living in Mali, Africa. They build their homes along cliffs near watering holes. They have developed a unique system of irrigation so they are able to plant crops such as rice and beans and even have goats and sheep. The villages have special granaries with straw roofs to protect their harvests and other goods. Higher on the cliffs are the Dogon cemeteries, which can only be reached with ladders.

▲ *The largest and most famous of the Anasazi cliff dwellings is called the Cliff Palace in Colorado. About 100 people lived in its 150 rooms. It also has 23 kivas. These round rooms were used for spiritual ceremonies.*

The Anasazi: Ancient Cliff Dwellers

Another group of cliff dwellers were the Anasazi people. Ancestors of the Pueblo people of today, they lived in the present-day states of Colorado, Arizona, New Mexico, and Utah. Thought to have lived in this region between the years 1200 BC and around 1300 AD, they built some of their stone homes in shallow caves or under cliff overhangs. Their cliff dwellings were made of blocks of hard sandstone held together with adobe mortar. Residents could only get to the homes by climbing up using small hand- and footholds carved into the walls. Sometimes there was a narrow rock bridge to cross with no handrails.

The Anasazi built their cliff dwellings facing the south so that the low winter Sun would heat their homes during the cold months. In the summer, the overhang would shade them from the Sun.

The cliffs were very steep, and the trails to the cliff homes were quite dangerous. Enemies who came to loot the Anasazi's food and supplies were in for a difficult climb.

► *The Iowa 80 truckstop on Interstate 80 in Walcott, Iowa, is the world's largest truckstop. It covers an area of 220 acres (89 hectares). Serving 5,000 customers each day, with space for 800 trucks, Iowa 80 has grown into a mini city for travelers offering food, shops, a movie theater, a barber, and even a dentist!*

FOCUS ON:

THE SILK ROAD

In ancient times, countries in Asia and the Middle East traded all kinds of products along routes that came to be known as the Silk Road. Fine silk fabric from China was traded for perfume, spices, and jewels. The routes were also used to transport gold, ivory, missionaries, and even slaves.

The Silk Road was not just one road. It was actually a network of routes that went both north and south of the Taklamakan Desert. The Romans tried to protect the route by building forts and outposts along it. Some of these grew to be large settlements with cultivated fields.

These routes not only moved goods, but also information, news, and cultures. It was, in great part, because of this exchange of ideas and products that the ancient civilizations of China, Egypt, Rome, and Persia grew to be such great centers of wealth and culture.

Stopping to Rest

In ancient times, important trade routes connected public markets and helped link producers with customers. As people moved goods from one place to another, they needed places to stop and rest and get supplies. Settlements often sprang up along these routes to provide for the caravans and the travelers.

Today we have highway systems that crisscross the countryside. Trucks and tankers haul everything from tissues to nuclear reactors. Along the way, like the traders of long ago, truckers need places to eat, rest, and fuel up. Truck stops, diners, and other rest areas offer truckers and other long-distance travelers some of the comforts they need to break up a tiring journey.

◄ *This artwork shows a caravan of merchants and camels traveling along the Silk Road through Asia.*

23

▲ *Niagara Falls, a wonder of nature that attracts visitors from all over the world. Some tourism surveys estimate that Niagara Falls receives between 20 million and 30 million visitors each year!*

Serving Those Who Travel

Wherever people gather, whether to look at an amazing waterfall, spend time at a summer resort, or enjoy the thrill of an amusement park, settlements usually spring up to provide products and services. Look at any tourist destination—chances are that some form of settlement has grown up around it.

Niagara Falls—A Magnet for Both Visitors and Residents

European explorers are believed to have first viewed Niagara Falls as early as 1604. Since the 1800s, hotels, restaurants, and shops have been built to cater to tourists who visit the waterfalls from all over the world. Today, permanent residents live on both sides of Niagara Falls, which straddles the border between Ontario, in Canada, and New York, in the United States. Parks, observation towers, pathways, and gardens let visitors enjoy the beauty of this area, while the towns and cities nearby provide for their comfort.

The Lure of Disney

In Florida, what was once only swampland was transformed in 1971 into a magical land of theme parks and rides based on the vision of Walt Disney. Sixty-six thousand people work at Walt Disney World, and millions of people visit the park each year. Two new cities were founded *inside* the property to help provide places for workers and visitors to live or stay. Restaurants, hotels, and medical services all around the park cater to the needs of tourists.

The Lure of Kilimanjaro

Mount Kilimanjaro is an inactive volcano in the African nation of Tanzania. It is the highest peak in Africa, and there are several hiking routes to the top of the mountain. Tourism has played a major part in the development of the towns surrounding the mountain.

Moshi is a small settlement at the base of Kilimanjaro. Many climbers stay in hotels in the area and hire local people to act as guides, porters, and cooks on their climbs. This is also the site of the Kilimanjaro Marathon. The course takes athletes through Moshi before leading them up the mountain for some breathtaking views, then sending them through banana and coffee plantations to the finish line.

▲ *Mount Kilimanjaro provides employment for many people who live around the base of the mountain. Here, a mountain guide and team of porters prepare to accompany visiting climbers to the summit of the mountain.*

▼ *The town of Moshi with Kilimanjaro in the distance.*

25

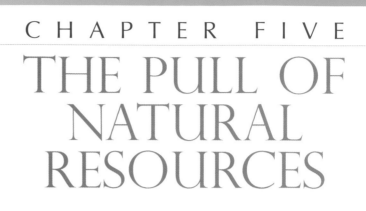

In Cornwall, in the west of England, tin mining was a major industry for many centuries. Many towns and villages grew up to house the miners. By the 1800s, overseas competition was making Cornish tin mining unprofitable. The mines were abandoned (as seen here), and many miners migrated overseas where their mining expertise was in great demand. Mining is in the Cornish blood, however, and today graduates from the Camborne School of Mines in Cornwall can be found working in mines from South Africa to Australia.

CHAPTER FIVE

THE PULL OF NATURAL RESOURCES

Many times the choice of location for a settlement has to do with the natural resources available to people. Historically, as civilizations grew they began to cultivate and store crops. With the means to put enough food aside to live on and be assured of continued nourishment, people could turn their attention to other things, such as taking care of shelter and clothing needs, developing crafts, industry and commerce, and leisure activities. All of these activities help create a sense of comfort and community within a settlement, and they almost always require the use of natural resources to make them happen.

▲ Nearly 2,000 years ago, the Romans created channels within the hills of Las Médulas, Spain, and used water pressure to force out gold deposits. This process caused the rock to collapse in ways that created the spectacular formations shown here.

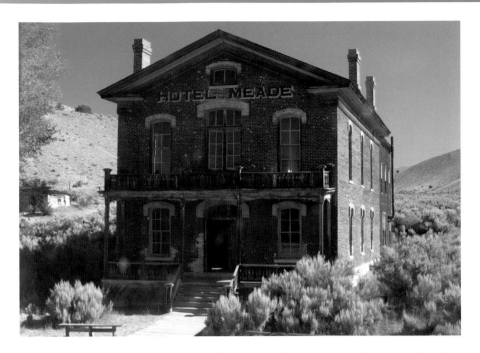

▲ *The abandoned Hotel Meade in Bannack, Montana. Today, as a National Historic Landmark, Bannack, although officially a ghost town, continues to provide a living for a small number of residents of nearby towns whose jobs depend on serving the people who come to visit and explore a real-life ghost town!*

Mining: Putting Nature to Work

Mining has always been an important industry around the world. In ancient times, huge stones were needed for buildings and statues. Metals were needed for tools and weapons to conquer other lands.

Gold and silver were mined in Spain and used to mint coins and make jewelry. Las Médulas in Spain was one of the biggest gold mines in the ancient Roman Empire. Around 2,000 years ago, the Romans built canals and waterways in the area in order to use water to wash the gold out of the rock. The village also had other advantages from the advanced Roman civilization, such as bathhouses with running water.

Settlements Based on Resources Today

Even today, new towns are being founded to provide homes, schools, and recreation for miners and their families. The Black Thunder coal mine in Wyoming is one of the largest in the United States and the nation's most productive. Wright, Wyoming, was founded in the 1970s to house the workers of the nearby coal mines. It started as a small community with mobile homes and one school but has grown to include many subdivisions of permanent homes, three schools, a golf course, sports facilities, and a recreation center with an Olympic-sized swimming pool.

GHOST TOWNS

Once a desired natural resource has been emptied from an area, the town that housed and supplied the workers might empty, too. People move on to find work somewhere else, and the thriving community becomes a ghost town.

Gold was discovered in Bannack, Montana, in 1896. The town swelled to 3,000 residents. The town had hotels, bakeries, blacksmith shops, stables, meat markets, a grocery store, a restaurant, a brewery, a billiard hall, and four saloons. When the gold dwindled, so did the population. The last residents left in the 1970s. Today, Bannack is a well-preserved ghost town that attracts many tourists.

Farming: A Vital Use of Our Resources

Since at least as far back as the time of the ancient Egyptians, farming has been a vital use of natural resources in order to provide enough food for Earth's growing population. Farming communities are often small, but they are in a central location where farmers can get supplies, sell their crops, and socialize.

Plants need fertile soil to grow, and livestock need healthy plants to eat. The most productive farms are on rich topsoil with a good climate. The perfect soil and location is not always available, however, so some farmers have had to be creative in how they use the land.

In the example shown earlier, farmers in the Yuanyang region of China found a way to plant crops up the slopes of mountains. They created terraces, or steps, up the sides and turned them into rice paddies.

▶ *A special irrigation system brings water even to the highest terraces that snake around the mountains in Yuanyang. Each farming village in this area has its own customs and traditional clothing. It is a very colorful sight when the villagers come together on market day to trade and socialize.*

JOURNEY STORIES

ALFRED G. McMICHAEL:

The gold rush in the Yukon Territory, in Canada, inspired thousands of men to travel north to seek their fortune. These men, called Stampeders, had a long and dangerous trek. They had to walk through snow and ice over mountains with narrow paths and jagged rocks. Avalanches, disease, and accidents claimed many lives. Alfred McMichael described the scene from along the Chilkoot Pass Trail in 1898:

I wish you could be here for a day or two just to see the busy scenes on the hills. It is impossible for me to describe them to you. Imagine a narrow trail over the snow, then crowd on it men with sleds, men with packs on their backs, dogs in trains of from two to eight, horses, mules and oxen, some drawing sleds and others with packs on their backs. All in an endless procession, going and coming. Now everything going smoothly, then all in confusion when some dogs get tangled up or a horse gets a little out of the trail and floundering up to his belly in the snow. They all toil up the hill...

Farming as an American Tradition

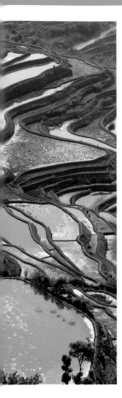

The U.S. Midwest is sometimes called the breadbasket of America because the flat, fertile ground is a good place to grow grains and corn. In the 1860s, the Homestead Act encouraged people to settle and farm in the West. Settlers were granted 160 acres (65 hectares) to farm. If, at the end of five years, they had lived on that land, built a home, farmed, and made improvements to the property, they would get the deed free and clear.

Many people ran to claim their free land, including immigrants from Scandinavia and other parts of Europe. The wind, blizzards, insects, and drought made growing and harvesting difficult. Out on the plains there were not many trees for building, and some homesteaders lived in what were called sod houses—homes made from slabs of soil and grass. Water and fuel were often scarce. The lack of fuel made cooking and heating difficult for the pioneers. By the time the Homestead Act was discontinued in the 1970s, 1.6 million homesteads had been granted, but many more were abandoned.

▼ *Twillingate is a town of fewer than 2,500 people on the northeastern coast of Newfoundland. Twillingate is a historic fishing community but today relies on tourism for much of its income.*

FISHING IN NEWFOUNDLAND

Fishing is an important natural resource. Oceans, lakes, and rivers not only provide food such as fish, shellfish, and seaweed, but also fertilizer, gems, and oil. It is no wonder that so many communities are located near water.

The island of Newfoundland in Canada was founded on the fishing industry. Fish merchants from the south of England and parts of France discovered the abundant fish resources in the 1700s. Merchants sent representatives to set up shops and temporary housing for their workers during the fishing season. Some fisherman decided to stay year round and built homes along the shores of the island.

The land in the interior of the island is too rocky and swampy for farming, so almost all the communities in Newfoundland are along the coasts. The only roads circle the edge of the island, and there are still some communities on the south shore that are not connected to the rest of the island by roads at all. They can still only be reached by boat.

AMERICAN INDIANS VERSUS AMERICAN SETTLERS ON THE OPENING OF THE WEST

Chief Joseph of the Nez Perce was opposed to signing the treaty with the United States giving up much of his band's land. His refusal, which he explains here in 1864, around the time of the passage of the Homestead Act, gave him the reputation of a humanitarian and peacemaker:

The first white men of your people who came to our country were named Lewis and Clark...They talked straight and our people gave them a great feast as proof that their hearts were friendly. For a short time we lived quietly. But this could not last. White men had found gold in the mountains around the land of the Winding Water. They stole a great many horses from us, and we could not get them back because we were Indians. We had no friends who would plead our cause before the law councils. It seemed to me that some of the white men in Wallowa were doing these things on purpose to get up a war. They knew we were not strong enough to fight them. I labored hard to avoid trouble and bloodshed. We gave up some of our country to the white men, thinking that then we could have peace.

John Hopkins was the son of the first postmaster in Douglas County, Missouri. Like many early settlers, he and his family lived in fear of the Native people:

Life was real and life was ernest (sic) in those days and also life was very insecure. Most of the Indians in this part of the country were friendly, but Indians were nomads and a settler never knew when some hostile band would move in and attempt to kill him and his home. Men wore rifles strapped to their backs while working in the fields. All the stock was driven in and fastened up at night because even a friendly Indian would steal livestock. As more settlers came in and the country became more thickly populated, these raids became fewer because retribution was swift.

Bring on the Machines!

In the 1700s, a new technology called steam power brought huge changes to the way people worked and lived. It meant that factories began to use machines rather than people or animals to do much of the work. It was called the Industrial Revolution.

In Great Britain, spinning and weaving with wheels and looms used to be done in farms and villages. With the invention of the spinning jenny and other machinery, spinning and weaving were now done in factories. This meant textiles could be made quickly and cheaply.

Mills had to be located near supplies of coal and running water, two resources that were plentiful in the north of England. Cities such as Manchester, Leeds, and Liverpool grew quickly as people came to work in the mills. Farming communities shrank as workers left to work in cities.

▼ *The Saltaire textile factory and town on the Leeds and Liverpool Canal near Bradford in England. The factory was founded in 1851 by businessman Titus Salt, who also provided homes, shops, and a library for his workers—but no taverns, as Salt did not drink alcohol!*

▲ *A large group of workers from a cotton mill in Tifton, Georgia. The younger members of the group are not the workers' children, but are in fact members of the mill's workforce.*

New Migratory Patterns

Steam power also caused a shift in where people settled. Using new steam engines to power machines instead of waterwheels meant that factories could be built in areas where waterpower wasn't available. New settlements sprang up to supply the factory with workers.

Pottery, crockery, and other craft items could be made in large quantities and became cheap and plentiful. Even ordinary workers could afford to buy them. Market towns grew larger, and more stores opened. New cities began to form, creating a greater need for services—and people to perform them.

Expanding Markets, Economies, and Populations

The increase in merchandise being produced and shipped meant that many port cities became larger, too. Port cities opened banking offices to handle the new trading center businesses. Ships would bring in cargo such as cotton, silk, dyes, and tea from countries in Asia. London, England, along with Amsterdam in the Netherlands and Hamburg in Germany, became important places of commerce as people and companies traded with the East Indies. These cities kept growing, even after the initial effects of the Industrial Revolution had begun to level off.

FOCUS ON:

CHILD LABOR

The move to the city from the countryside during the Industrial Revolution did not always mean a better life for families. People settled near the factories, but the housing was crowded and small. The wages from factory work were often low, and many families found themselves without enough money to pay for food, shelter, or clothing. Children were often sent to work to help the family situation. Children worked in factories and mines and as chimney sweeps. Small children could scramble under machinery to get cotton bobbins or crawl in tiny spaces in mines. Some children started to work as young as five years old. Many were seriously injured or killed.

Amsterdam is still the financial center of the Netherlands. The Amsterdam Stock Exchange in the city center is the oldest stock exchange in the world. Several of the world's biggest companies have their headquarters there.

London today has 480 banks from other countries in the city limits. Its port was once the busiest in the world. It is a major center for international business.

Hamburg is still an important port for central Europe. It is also a major location for shipyards and shipbuilding.

Early Misery in the Americas

In some areas of the world, the population grew, shrank, and changed many times, as different groups inhabited different parts of the globe. One region that underwent significant changes almost from the moment the first European set foot on its soil in 1492 was the Caribbean.

▼ Sugarcane, shown here being harvested in recent years on the island of St. Kitts, was a natural resource that became the basis for much of the British slave trade in the Caribbean.

◀ *This model shows a traditional Taino settlement and large communal hut.*

The Caribbean contains thousands of islands, big and small. At the time that Europeans first arrived in the Americas, different tribes lived on the islands. One of the main tribes were the Taino. They grew most of their food but also hunted and fished. The center of their community was an open space, or plaza, that they used for ceremonies, games, and festivals. Their houses were large round huts made of wooden poles, straw, and palm leaves. Up to 15 families might live in one building.

Spain Puts in Its Claim

Christopher Columbus arrived in the Caribbean while trying to find a direct passage to Asia. Spain claimed the islands that he touched foot on and set about to conquer the indigenous people. Some were sent back to Spain as slaves, and others were forced to work on the islands in the gold mines. Native people who refused to work were often killed, and many more died of the diseases that the Spanish carried. Soon, there were hardly any Native people left, and their settlements were abandoned. The Spanish then imported slaves from Africa to work on the islands.

Britain and France Stake Their Claim

Britain and France also claimed some of the islands. The British realized that these islands had the perfect climate to grow sugarcane. They set up huge sugar plantations and brought more slaves to work them. Slavery was finally abolished throughout the Americas at various times during the 1800s, and the Africans were free to settle and work. There were no urban areas on the islands where they could find jobs in factories or offices. The only jobs were on the plantations where European companies controlled the wages.

Starting in the 1800s many of the islands gained their independence from Europe. The main industry in this area is now tourism. Ports have been built to accommodate large cruise ships, and towns and villages nearby sell handicrafts and souvenirs.

PIRATES SETTLING IN THE CARIBBEAN

Nassau, an island in the Caribbean group known as the Bahamas, was once home to many pirates. It started out as just a collection of tents and taverns, but it grew into a thriving pirate community. The many secluded coves and bays were perfect places for pirate ships to lie in wait for passing Spanish galleons loaded with gold and silver. One of the most famous residents was the pirate Blackbeard (above). It was from here that he sailed aboard his ship *Queen Anne's Revenge* and terrorized the Caribbean.

◀ *A cruise ship in harbor during a tour of the Caribbean. Today, the climate, blue ocean, and scenery in this part of the world mean the islands' many cities and towns are able to earn their living from tourism.*

▼ Ships use only about one-tenth of the fuel that trucks would need, so they are easier on the environment. One container ship can carry as much cargo as hundreds of trucks.

CHAPTER SIX

TRANSPORTATION LINKS

Cities and towns around the world are often located by rivers, oceans, or other large bodies of water, such as the Great Lakes. These locations were not only important in order for people to be close to sources of food or water, but also for transportation. Transportation is vital for trade, and trade is vital for the wealth of a country. All the major ancient civilizations were founded on large rivers or a seacoast. Travel by water was generally faster and cheaper than most ways of traveling on land, and water was a resource that was usually in good supply and didn't need any upkeep!

▲ A horse tows a sailboat along the Barton Aqueduct, in Manchester, England. The aqeuduct opened in 1761 and was used to convey the Bridgewater Canal over the River Irwell. The aqueduct was later demolished during the building of new waterways.

▲ *Niagara Falls was a barrier to ships on the St. Lawrence River getting to the Great Lakes. The Welland Canal was built so ships could go around the falls, using eight locks that lift the ships almost 328 feet (100 m). Here, a large cargo ship enters Lock 3 of the Welland Canals System in St. Catharines, Ontario.*

The Wonder of Canals

Water transportation systems were not only important for trading goods but also for trading information. The most advanced civilizations were the ones that could share ideas and inventions with other cultures.

Where a natural waterway didn't exist, people found a way to build one. Canals and locks are artificial waterways that link lakes, rivers, and oceans.

The Bridgewater Canal in northwest England was built in the late 1700s to help transport coal from the mines to Manchester. This cut the cost of the coal in half, and suddenly canals were being built all over England. During this time of "canal mania," roughly 100 canals were built. Towns and villages sprang up all along the canal system as it provided a cheap and simple way to move products and people.

The St. Lawrence Seaway, which is part of the border between Canada and the United States, uses both natural and manmade waterways to form a marine "highway" that is 2,300 miles (3,700 km) long. There are 41 ports along the way, which connect to rail lines and roadways to deliver all kinds of products. Millions of people live along the St. Lawrence Seaway and take advantage of the goods and services that it helps deliver.

Enter the Railroad

Railroads were a turning point in the development of many countries. Before the modern era of trains in the 1800s, travel on land was difficult and slow. Trains allowed the expansion and settlement of land far away from waterways.

Before the railroad, the American West was a vast prairie. The grasslands were home to herds of buffalo and the Native people who hunted them. Settlers making their way across the continent struggled with difficult weather, harsh growing conditions, and conflicts with Native people.

Work on the Transcontinental Railroad, which was completed in 1869, was mostly done by Chinese and Irish immigrants. The work was dangerous, and many lost their lives, but most of those who survived settled in the United States.

Westward Ho!

The railroads encouraged people to settle in the West. They promoted communities, sold land, and provided jobs for many people. They advertised in Europe with pamphlets telling prospective settlers about the climate, the natural resources, jobs, and schools. The railroad even ran special "land-seeking" trains, and if the passenger decided to buy land, the price of the train ticket was subtracted from the price of the land.

▶ This artwork shows a buffalo hunting expedition conducted from a train. Groups of wealthy Europeans were able to take a trip on which they would ride through herds of buffalo taking potshots at them. This helped lead to the destruction of the buffalo herds on the plains.

JOURNEY STORIES

JAMES (MADISON) COON AND NANCY (INESS) COON:

The journey to the American West was very difficult and dangerous. One out of every ten people died along the way. Some walked the whole distance barefoot. The biggest challenges along the way were not the Native people, but disease and accidents. James Madison and Nancy Iness were married in 1847. Only two months later they began their journey west along the Oregon Trail:

Camped at a Sioux Indian town. Quite a trade was got up between the women and Squaws trading beads and other trinkets for bread and meat. At Fort Laramie the old Chief told us we had to pay him for passing through his country. The commander at the Post told us it was customary to give him something. He spread down his blanket and each man put on his pay, some flour, some meat, coffee, beans, peas, dried fruit, etc. He was well pleased.

Left the river after coming down it four miles (6.4 km). Came seven miles (11 km) and left the road, went one mile (1.6 km) to the river and camped. Grass and wood are scarce. I lost two of my oxen, Jack and Jerry. A few Indians standing around offered to hunt them down for two shirts but I hunted for them until I got so tired hunting I could go no further. Then I accepted their offer, whereupon they mounted their ponies. Presently they returned with the oxen and I finished the bargain by giving them two shirts.

▶ As far back as 2,000 years ago, ancient Romans were paving roadways in their Empire with smooth, level stones and concrete so they would last a long time and not need many repairs. These roads made it possible to move armies and supplies quickly from town to town. This paved section of road (right) is in the ruined Roman city of Pompeii in Italy.

At the time, Baltimore was the biggest immigrant pier in the United States. Immigrants who came from overseas were often sold a train ticket west along with their ship passage.

Many people settled near the rail line. The closer a farmer was to a railroad, the easier it was to ship his crops and livestock to market. The railroad companies were eager to help the new settlers, too. They supported agricultural improvements because they knew that if farmers had crops to sell, they would need a way to transport them. So the more successful farmers were, the more successful the railroad company would also be.

Smoothing the Way on Land

Rivers and railroads were not the only methods of transportation that encouraged settlement. Dirt tracks and cobblestone lanes became paved roads. The major routes were turned into smooth, safe highways, letting people travel to places that rivers and railways didn't go.

The Trans-Canada Highway: World's Longest

The Trans-Canada Highway is the longest national highway in the world. It starts in St. John's, Newfoundland, at the Atlantic Ocean and runs right across Canada to Victoria, British Columbia, on the Pacific Ocean. It is 4,860 miles (7,821 km) long. Thirty major communities as well as countless small towns and villages line the route. All along are places for travelers to eat, sleep, and enjoy some entertainment.

▲ A map showing the route of the Trans-Canada Highway across Canada.

ROAD TRAINS

Many countries rely on trucks to bring goods to different areas. Australia has many remote communities that are only accessible by road. Supplies are often brought to these places by road trains (as above). These are trucks with more than one trailer behind. Some trucks pull as many as four trailers or tankers and are called "quads." The road trains bring everything from fuel to livestock to general supplies.

Australia's Cross-Country Highway

The Stuart Highway in Australia crosses the middle of the continent. It follows the route of John McDouall Stuart, the first European to travel overland from the south coast to the north. It takes seven days to travel from one end to the other. It has brought many tourists to the area as the route winds its way past famous landmarks such as Uluru, Alice Springs, and the mining town of Coober Pedy.

More Ways to Get from Here to There: Ferries

Towns and cities today are found in places that used to be too difficult to reach. In order for the communities to grow, they need access to services and supplies.

Ferries are boats that carry passengers and their vehicles across water. Some larger ferries carry trucks and even railroad cars. Running ferries on the water is cheaper than building tunnels under water or bridges over water. Ferries are also used on the world's busiest seaway, the English Channel. This body of water is the link between Great Britain and the rest of Europe. Some ferries that cross here daily carry mostly tourists. Others are used for freight.

Ice Roads

Many northern countries use ice roads to reach remote settlements in the winter. These frozen highways are built over water. They are created when the ice is thick enough to support the weight of trucks and cars. Many times ferries can't run in the winter because the river or lake is frozen. In some places, ice roads keep supplies running to communities.

In Sweden, ice roads connect the mainland with islands in winter, bringing food and fuel to remote settlements. There are many limits on traveling these roads. Vehicles must be under a certain weight, they cannot travel too close together, and they must not stop. Drivers can only use them in daylight and are not allowed to wear seat belts. If they are strapped in and the ice gives way, they might become trapped in their car and drown in the icy water.

In Canada, the ice road in the Northwest Territories was vital to the building of Canada's diamond mines. It is only open eight to ten weeks a year, from February to April, and must be rebuilt every winter. It crosses over 75 lakes and ponds. The speed on the ice road is carefully controlled to protect the ice. The Diavik Diamond mine brings in about 2,500 truckloads of supplies each season.

▲ The Channel Tunnel runs under the English Channel connecting England and France. Travelers cross under the ocean in trains including large trains (as seen above) that carry cars and trucks. The car and truck drivers simply drive onto the train, switch off their engines, and enjoy the ride.

▼ A truck drives along the ice highway to Tuktoyaktuk, in the Northwest Territories, Canada.

CHAPTER SEVEN

URBANIZATION AND SUBURBANIZATION

The terms *urbanization* **and** *suburbanization* **refer to patterns of human migration and settlement that are common in virtually every part of the world where large numbers of people live in a relatively small area. One pattern, urbanization, refers to people migrating into cities. The other, suburbanization, refers to people migrating out of the cities and into outlying areas that have grown up around the cities.**

A Variety of Factors

Each pattern is related to a variety of factors that influence human migration and settlement. These factors include the availability of jobs, economic needs such as affordable housing, social concerns such as safety and convenience of travel and shopping, and environmental concerns such as climate and the quality of air and water.

Starting Off Small . . .

Nearly every major city in North America started out as a trading post where Europeans bought, sold, and bartered animal furs and other items with Native people and with each other. This pattern of settlement is especially reflected in the growth of cities up and down the seacoasts, around the Great Lakes, and along the major rivers in North America.

◀ *An aerial view of a housing development near Markham, Ontario, Canada. Designed mostly during the growth of suburbs in the 1950s, such developments were commonly known as tract housing.*

▲ *Kuala Lumpur, the capital of Malaysia, may be seen looming over the urban sprawl that has developed as suburbs and commuter towns beyond the city's original boundaries.*

. . . And Growing

With the growth of business and industry along these natural aquatic trade routes came more jobs and greater numbers of people migrating in search of work. Settlements grew into small towns, and small towns became the large cities they are today, such as New York, Montreal, Chicago, and Detroit. These increasing populations required the kinds of services that in turn lead to more jobs and more people migrating to the area. These services include health care, education, construction, transportation, and utilities.

▼ *This view of Rio de Janeiro, Brazil, dramatically shows the stark distinction between the city's gleaming skyline and the overcrowded, poverty-stricken shantytowns, called favelas, on the city's outskirts.*

Into the Cities . . .

Population patterns are constantly changing. In newly industrialized countries factories are bringing people from the countryside into the cities. Cities such as Thane, in India, have grown rapidly to accommodate the new residents. Thane has a large section where there are chemical, engineering, textile, and electrical industries.

In many countries, new migrants find that they cannot afford decent housing in the cities into which they have moved. Some may not even be able to find jobs. In most Western nations, such as the United Kingdom and United States, these people tend to stay in the cities, where their transportation costs are still low. In cases where their housing may be less expensive, in large part this is so because it may also be of poor quality. These areas become the inner-city slums and poor neighborhoods that characterize so many cities in North America.

CITY LIVING VS. COUNTRY LIVING

City dweller Nguyen cites many reasons why he likes living in an urban setting:

In a city, there are many facilities for recreation as well as heath care. For example, we can find a large number of shops in which we can buy daily goods at (a) low price right in our neighborhood. Besides, (for) people concerned) most about their health and safety, medical facilities and emergency services are more accessible than those in the country. Therefore, city life is more convenient than village life. Big cities also offer efficient public transport and high-speed Internet access as well as complete social services.

Benedict disagrees. He describes what he loves best about country living:

First (thing) that comes to mind is that the countryside is a breath of fresh air, literally and figuratively. Air is cleaner here than (in) the city. On top of that, (there are fewer) crimes in the countryside. It is also more likely for a person to establish good relationships with his or her neighbors as people in the countryside are more friendly, caring, and true. The cost of living in the country is considerably cheaper than the city.

▲ Huge suburban housing developments such as this one in Calgary, Alberta, Canada, have many streets ending in circular dead ends called cul de sacs and are often difficult to reach from outside of the development. Some people feel that these features needlessly isolate suburban dwellers from the communities around them.

. . . And Out of the Cities

In developing countries such as India and the Philippines, the search for jobs has also led to rapid urbanization. In these nations, as in Western nations, many people have found that they could not afford housing. However, in places such as Brazil and Kenya, migrants in this situation typically find themselves forced to move outside of the city centers. There, they live in overcrowded slums and "shantytowns" where conditions are characterized by extreme poverty and overcrowding. These slums usually also lack clean water and other basic services such as sewers.

New Migratory Patterns

In industrialized countries such as Canada, the United States, and the United Kingdom, population patterns have been quite changeable. Following a century or more of movement into the cities as mechanized, mass production led to the creation of factories in urban areas, the centers of many big cities have become crowded and housing has become more expensive. Air quality in most cities tends to be poor, and crime may be on the rise. Over the last few decades, many people living in these areas have left the city centers. Most people still depend on the cities for their source of income, supplies, and entertainment. However, those who can afford to commute in and out of cities have moved into suburban towns.

Today, with technology making long-distance jobs a reality, people are free to live farther from the offices and factories found in large cities. This has led to yet more people discovering that they can work away from cities, often in their homes, where they can "telecommute" via phone and the Internet. These circumstances have provided yet one more set of reasons that suburban populations have grown in recent decades while city-center populations are shrinking.

Back to the Cities!

In another twist on the patterns of migration in and around cities, the migration of people to the suburbs—along with a poor housing market— has driven down the cost of housing in many cities. In these places, the cost of living in cities may actually be decreasing, making it more affordable for people to move closer to jobs and to the cultural and recreational advantages of being around movie theaters, museums, and restaurants. Concerns about pollution from commuting and efforts by cities to improve buildings and parks in inner city areas are also making it more desirable for people to move back.

Many urban planners, politicians, and citizens are hoping that the coming decades may see the reawakening and revitalization of life in the cities. Time will tell whether this will be a short-lived trend or a sustained pattern for generations to come.

▲ These steppers from the Bronx, New York, are performing at an outdoor arts event. Despite the rigors of urban life, cities provide enriching experiences for those who live, work, and grow up in their neighborhoods.

▲ Left: Freeway construction and the moving of many residents and businesses to the suburbs or other parts of town left these buildings disused and boarded up in the Third Ward warehouse district of Milwaukee. Right: After several years of rehabbing those same buildings. The Third Ward is home to apartments, condos, restaurants, nightclubs, theaters, art galleries, museums, shops, and even a microbrewery.

GLOSSARY

45th parallel north A circle of latitude 45 degrees north of the equator, thought of as approximately halfway between the equator and the North Pole and designating the southernmost extent of the most recent descent of glaciers

archaeologist A scientist who studies history by excavating and analyzing sites, ruins, artifacts, and other remains of past people and civilizations

archipelago A chain or cluster of many small islands

bartered Traded

canal An artificial waterway built for shipping or irrigation

climate Weather conditions in one area over a long period of time

commerce The business of buying and selling goods and services

communal Shared for use by members of a group

continental shelf The shallow part of the ocean floor that surrounds continents

cultivated Prepared (as in soil) to grow crops

delta an area, usually roughly shaped like a triangle, made up of minute particles, called sediment, that flows down the course of a river and collects at its mouth

drought A long period of time with no rain

East Indies A group of thousands of islands between the mainland of Southeast Asia and Australia, including all or portions of the nations of Indonesia, Malaysia, the Philippines, Singapore, East Timor, Papua New Guinea, and Brunei. Historically, the East Indies have also included South and Southeast Asia extending from India and Pakistan eastward.

Eurasia The landmass of Europe and Asia together

galleon A large sailing ship with three or more masts; used by the Spanish

geologic Also geological; having to do with the physical features of the planet, such as rocks and land formations

glacial period Time during an ice age when the glaciers are moving and growing

glacier A slow-moving mass of ice formed by the compression of snow and ice near the poles

global warming The gradual increase in the average temperature of Earth's atmosphere over time due to the accumulation of heat-retaining gases, known as greenhouse gases, in the atmosphere

High Arctic Areas north of the Arctic Circle

ice ages Long periods when the temperature of Earth's surface and atmosphere is reduced; marked by glacial periods and the appearance of glaciers and ocean sheets of ice

irrigate To supply dry land with water using ditches, canals, or pipes

latitude The distance north or south of Earth's equator, usually measured in units called degrees and minutes

missionaries People who travel to foreign countries to promote their religion

Nomads Groups that do not settle in one area but move from place to place, usually in response to seasonal or climatic changes

northern hemisphere The half of the planet that is north of the equator

oasis A fertile spot in a desert at or near a source of water

opal A gemstone of a mineral that comes in many colors

outback The wilderness region in the interior of Australia

polar regions The areas around the North and South Poles

rain forest A forest with a heavy yearly rainfall and warm temperatures

silt Deposits of sediment at the bottom of a river or lake

stock exchange An organized market for buying and selling stocks and bonds

subarctic Of or having to do with areas just south of the Arctic Circle

subcontinent A large landmass, such as that made up by India, Pakistan, and Bangladesh

sub-Saharan South of the Sahara Desert

terraced Made up of a series of level shelves of land forming a slope and resembling stairs

textiles Cloth made by weaving, felting, or knitting

urban Having to do with cities or towns

utilities Public services that include electricity, water, gas, or sewers

West Bank A region between Israel and Jordan on the west bank of the Jordan River; home to millions of Palestinians, occupied by Israel since the Six Day War of 1967, and one of the territories considered the basis for a future Palestinian state

IDEAS FOR DISCUSSION

- Using the Internet and the library, trace the history of the area in which you live. Why did the first settlers locate here? What natural resources or human resources did the location offer? Why did your family settle here?

- Make a list of capital cities from around the world. Why do you think these settlements became such powerful sites? Discuss what factors most capital cities have in common in terms of resources, location, or transportation?

- Using maps, the Internet, and your own knowledge of world geography, pick an unpopulated area in the world and plan a new settlement there. What sorts of resources does this location offer? What kinds of adaptations will the residents need to make in order to live here? What kinds of businesses or industries will the community as a whole need in order to prosper and grow in this area? Based on the settlement's location, land formation, and climate, what environmental concerns would this settlement have?

- What kinds of resources (natural or human) are becoming more important in today's society? Which areas of the world are rich or poor in these resources? Which towns or cities do you predict will struggle or thrive because of these factors?

FURTHER INFORMATION

www.bradshawfoundation.com/stephenoppenheimer/

The Bradshaw Foundation is devoted to preserving ancient rock art around the world. You can follow The Journey of Mankind with the interactive map and see images of the artwork of early humans from around the world.

anthropology.uwaterloo.ca/ArcticArchStuff/index.html

Arctic North America has been home to some of the most amazing adaptations of humans anywhere. The University of Waterloo Arctic Archaeology site gives fascinating information on current dig sites and the newest discoveries.

www.kidspast.com/index.php

This site takes you on a tour of world history. Learn about prehistoric humans, great civilizations, and ancient America.

www.postalmuseum.si.edu/gold/gold.html

This site, created by the National Postal Museum, offers first-hand accounts from the Klondike/Alaskan gold rush, the last of the great gold rushes in the 1800s. Learn about female stampeders and what it was like to "run the rapids" down the Yukon River.

INDEX

INDEX

ABOUT THE AUTHOR

*Natalie Hyde graduated from the University of Waterloo with an Honors
Degree in Languages. She writes fiction and nonfiction for children and young adults.
Her middle-grade novel, Saving Armpit, is her fiction debut.
Natalie lives with her husband and four children.*